Keep this pocket-sized
you are travelling arou

Whether you are in your car or on foot, you will
enjoy an evocative journey back in time. Compare
the Lancashire of old with what you can see today
—examine how the cities, towns and villages have
changed down the years, how shops and buildings
have been altered or replaced; inspect fine details
such as lamp-posts, shop fascias and trade signs.

See the many alterations to the Lancashire landscape that have taken place during our lives, and
which we may have taken for granted. At the turn
of a page you will gain fascinating insights into
Lancashire's unique history.

FRANCIS FRITH'S
pocket ALBUM

HEART OF LANCASHIRE

A POCKET ALBUM

Adapted from an original book by
CLIFF HAYES

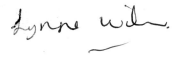

First published in the United Kingdom in 2004 by
Frith Book Company Ltd

Paperback edition
ISBN 1-85937-884-6

British Library Cataloguing in Publication Data

Heart of Lancashire—A Pocket Album
Adapted from an original book by Cliff Hayes

Frith Book Company Ltd
Frith's Barn, Teffont,
Salisbury, Wiltshire SP3 5QP
Tel: +44 (0) 1722 716 376
Email: info@francisfrith.co.uk
www.francisfrith.co.uk

Printed and bound in Great Britain by MPG, Bodmin

Front Cover: Downham, The Post Office and Old Stocks 1921 71190

The colour-tinting is for illustrative purposes only, and is not intended to be historically accurate.

Frontispiece: Clitheroe, Market Place 1921 71131

CONTENTS

FRANCIS FRITH
VICTORIAN PIONEER

Francis Frith, founder of the world-famous photographic archive, was a complex and multi-talented man. A devout Quaker and a highly successful Victorian businessman, he was philosophical by nature and pioneering in outlook. By 1855 he had already established a wholesale grocery business in Liverpool, and sold it for the astonishing sum of £200,000, which is the equivalent today of over £15,000,000. Now in his thirties, and captivated by the new science of photography, Frith set out on a series of pioneering journeys up the Nile and to the Near East.

INTRIGUE AND EXPLORATION

He was the first photographer to venture beyond the sixth cataract of the Nile. Africa was still the mysterious 'Dark Continent', and Stanley and Livingstone's historic meeting was a decade into the future. The conditions for picture taking confound belief. He laboured for hours in his wicker dark-room in the sweltering heat of the desert, while the volatile chemicals fizzed dangerously in their trays. Back in London he exhibited his photographs and was 'rapturously cheered' by members of the Royal Society. His reputation as a photographer was made overnight.

VENTURE OF A LIFE-TIME

By the 1870s the railways had threaded their way across the country, and Bank Holidays and half-day Saturdays had been made obligatory by Act of Parliament. All of a sudden the working man and his family were able to enjoy days out, take holidays, and see a little more of the world.

With typical business acumen, Francis Frith foresaw that these new tourists would enjoy having souvenirs to commemorate their days out. For the next thirty years he travelled the country by train and by pony and trap, producing fine photographs of seaside resorts and beauty spots that were keenly bought by millions of Victorians. These prints were painstakingly pasted into family albums and pored over during the dark nights of winter, rekindling precious memories of summer excursions. Frith's studio was soon supplying retail shops all over the country, and by 1890 F Frith & Co had become the greatest specialist photographic publishing company in the world, with over 2,000 sales outlets, and pioneered the picture postcard.

FRANCIS FRITH'S LEGACY

Francis Frith had died in 1898 at his villa in Cannes, his great project still growing. The archive he created continued in business for another seventy years. By 1970 it contained over a third of a million pictures showing 7,000 British towns and villages.

Frith's legacy to us today is of immense significance and value, for the magnificent archive of evocative photographs he created provides a unique record of change in the cities, towns and villages throughout Britain over a century and more. Frith and his fellow studio photographers revisited locations many times down the years to update their views, compiling for us an enthralling and colourful pageant of British life and character.

We are fortunate that Frith was dedicated to recording the minutiae of everyday life. For it is this sheer wealth of visual data, the painstaking chronicle of changes in dress, transport, street layouts, buildings, housing, engineering and landscape that captivates us so much today, offering us a powerful link with the past and with the lives of our ancestors.

Computers have now made it possible for Frith's many thousands of images to be accessed almost instantly. The archive offers every one of us an opportunity to examine the places where we and our families have lived and worked down the years. Its images, depicting our shared past, are now bringing pleasure and enlightenment to millions around the world a century and more after his death.

HEART OF LANCASHIRE
AN INTRODUCTION

LANCASHIRE is a wonderful county, the very best one of all. Ask any Lancastrian: they will tell you the truth! Lancashire has many faces, and Lancastrians are so big-hearted that you would think they have more than one heart. People who think of Lancashire as consisting of just grim industrial towns have never seen the sweeping beauty of the moorlands. Those who holiday at her coastal resorts are balanced by those who get pleasure and relaxation by walking on Pendle and the other hills at the very heart of the county.

Lancashire people are like the county: they have hidden depths, and there are more sides to them than most people. A Lancashire man will fight his corner with the tenacity of a Manchester terrier, but he will soften and help you once he has won. A Lancashire lady can be full of fun, but when things go wrong she has the world's best advice and a cup of tea. Lancashire people have a wonderful dry sense of humour and an ability to laugh at themselves. While in other areas people 'take the mickey' and poke fun at each other, in Lancashire they laugh with you, not at you. Sarcastic they may be, but they are gentle with it.

This book is a collection of memories from both sides of the heart of Lancashire. Firstly we see the villages of the Ribble Valley, an area of outstanding beauty, and we follow the Ribble and Hodder from the Yorkshire border down to Preston. Then we turn south and go into the industrial heartland. There we find the coal mining area, the very centre of Lancashire, that did so much for the war effort; and the cotton area, with its large mills.

I think we are very fortunate that the Frith team has covered this area so well in the past. They have recorded very thoroughly an area that is often seen as being off the beaten track. I was faced with over one hundred great photographs of the towns and villages in and around the Ribble Valley and the heart of Lancashire, and I wondered how to attack the problem. Alphabetically, the book would jump all over the place, so I thought that perhaps I should go from north to south – I was not sure. Then it dawned on me that every one of these villages and towns was on water. Whether it was stream, burn, water, river or even the Leeds to Liverpool canal, every town and village was next to some water. So I have laid the book out following the rivers of the area. Just as ancient man did, so this volume follows the rivers from upstream down. I hope that you agree with our choice of photographs, and that you have a pleasant journey down the streams.

Our book shows views and scenes that have not been in print for many years. I hope the book makes you visit the area to see the secrets of Lancashire. Visit the Trough of Bolland and Pendle – these are truly areas of unspoilt beauty, and are hidden gems in the very heart of Lancashire.

Here we see the pack-horse bridge at Hurst Green. The newer road bridge, built in 1826, is behind it. Clitheroe and Great Mitton are to the right, and Stoneyhurst to the left. The bridge was built in the 1500s at a cost of £70, and was paid for by Richard Sherburne, lord of the manor. It is still there today.

On the River Hodder: High in the Hills

The name Hodder means 'pleasant stream'. It is a Celtic name, and it describes the river well. Rising on Lamb Hill Fell, the river now runs into the Stock Reservoir and then resumes its wandering in North Lancashire. In an area dominated by rivers, crossing them has always been a problem. The smaller rivers were crossed on planks and stepping stones. Then came fords: cutting the banks to widen rivers makes them shallow enough to drive or walk across. However, the need to be able to cross in all weathers, at all times of the year, meant bridges had to be built. One of the most famous of the area's bridges, and certainly one of the oldest on the Hodder, is near Hurst Green (Stoneyhurst).

RIVER HODDER

THE BRIDGES 1894 / 34339A

9

Now very much part of Lancashire, the village of Slaidburn was in Yorkshire at the time of our photograph. 'Slaid' means 'flat marshy ground', 'burn' is the Old English word for brook, so the name means 'flat marshy ground by the brook', which describes the area well. The Black Bull public house on the left was later to become a Youth Hostel. This is where Church Street meets Chapel Street. On the right we see the famous Hark to Bounty Inn, which was used as an area court house.

SLAIDBURN

CHURCH STREET 1921 / 71212

Slaidburn nestles in a hollow with higher ground around it. As well as the River Hodder at the east of the village, it has Crossdale Brook running through it. Just before it enters the village, the brook runs over a weir which was built to keep the water deeper for a mill that was here two centuries ago. It was at Slaidburn that many of the ancient pack-horse trails used to meet or cross. Here we see the outskirts of Slaidburn.

SLAIDBURN

TOWN END c1955 / S139007

This is the most northerly of all the photographs in our book. Hammerton Hall lies in a crook of the River Hodder, with a stream called Barn Gill and its waterfall in the grounds. The bridge in the foreground is over the Barn Gill. Hammerton Hall is really an enlarged and fortified farmhouse.

SLAIDBURN

HAMMERTON HALL 1921 / 71217

This lovely view was taken just a few miles north of Dunsop Bridge. We can see the tiny River Brennand running down to join the Whitendale River to make the River Dunsop, which gives the town its name. The Ordnance Survey department has declared Dunsop Bridge to be the village nearest to the exact centre of the British Isles.

DUNSOP BRIDGE

BRENNAND VALLEY 1921 / 71231

This splendid view of the River Hodder shows the magnificent scenery of the area. The photograph shows the scene as it could have been 100 years earlier, except for the gas pipe crossing the river in the bottom left-hand corner. Hidden among the trees in the centre of our photograph is a foot (and animal) bridge just a few miles outside Dunsop Bridge. The hill on the left is called Knot or Sugar Loaf.

DUNSOP BRIDGE
THE HODDER BRIDGE 1921 / 71220

When our photograph was taken, Whitewell really was just a small and remote community. Being so near the old Roman road from Manchester to York, and being so well-placed on many routes, it has always had a reputation for putting up visitors and travellers. There was once a royal hunting forest next to Whitewell, and that brought in the aristocracy of past times.

WHITEWELL

1921 / 71245

This road that threads its way through the village is the A59 from Clitheroe to Skipton. The village policeman in his cape stands talking. In 1260 a charter was granted to hold a fair in Gisburn. The width of the street shows that the village was laid out with room for the country market that was once held here, with stalls on the cobbles either side. Some of the cottages go back to the 1500s.

The River Ribble and above Clitheroe

The River Ribble is one of the major rivers in the north-west of England. It rises on the border with Yorkshire, and tumbles down the hillsides to meet up with the River Hodder and the River Calder to gather strength before pushing on to Preston and the coast. This area where the three rivers meet is one that has sustained life since man arrived in the area. The fact that there are so many streams and burns feeding into the river system makes the area even more fascinating. Every village has a river or a stream; the water was so pure that it was the drinking water, the ale and the washing machine of the community.

GISBURN

MAIN STREET 1921 / 71203

The name of the village had an 'e' on the end until the railway company put up their sign spelt 'Gisburn', and the 'e' was forgotten. Here we see the main street. Once a year the village would be packed with visitors; they came to lean over Paythorne Bridge and watch the salmon leaping in the River Ribble. Salmon Sunday was still popular into the 1960s, and it is making a revival today. One of the Lister family built Gisburn Hall and Gisburn Park. Now a hospital, it was later the home of the Ribblesdale family.

GISBURN

MAIN STREET 1921 / 71202

This is a charming photograph of the area outside the churchyard entrance. Many refer to this village as the most perfect in Lancashire, with its village green next to the church, and old inn. In the church is the famous Pudsay Chapel: the large local marble lid of Sir Ralph Pudsay's tomb has carvings of himself and his three wives and his twenty-five children. The church is dedicated to St Peter and St Paul. Its history is unique, for a king helped in its design. Henry VI is said to have lived here in Bolton Hall for a year or so while hiding from the Yorkists in 1464 after losing the Battle of Hexham.

BOLTON BY BOWLAND

THE CHURCH GATES 1921 / 71208

We see the Green from the far side. The village (the name means 'the dwelling by the bow of the river') has two greens; because it was all part of the Pudsay estate, there was no pressure to expand or to pull down and rebuild. The right-hand side of the building at the end of the path was at one time the old Court House. You can tell it by the larger first-floor windows: they let in more light for the Lord of the Manor and the visiting judges, as they sat and listened to cases concerning the Forrest and Trough law.

BOLTON BY BOWLAND

THE GREEN 1921 / 71206

Barnoldswick is pronounced 'Barlick' by the locals. This is another village that has moved with boundary changes. It has been in Yorkshire longer than in Lancashire, but Lancashire is where it is now—so we can include it. Do not shout too loud about it, though, as there are many locals who would rather it were back across the border. Tubber Hill is on the outskirts of Barnoldswick; running alongside it is part of the Roman road which once went from Preston to York.

BARNOLDSWICK

TUBBER HILL c1920 / B589004

BARNOLDSWICK

CHURCH STREET 1952 / B589011

Church Street leads down to St. Mary-le-Gill Church. It was built around 1160 on the edge of the town by Cistercian monks, who found the natives not very friendly when they tried to establish an abbey here in 1147. The Commercial Hotel can be seen on the left, with two local men passing the time of day. Savage's and Burton's Menswear shop are on the right, and there is a cafe further up the street.

Barnoldswick grew once the Leeds-Liverpool canal arrived around 1812.
The local textile industry blossomed, and people moved into the village from
the surrounding areas to work in the new mills. Quarries sprang up, and jobs
were created. Here we see a section of the canal at Greenberfield Locks, just
before it enters the town. This is the highest point that the canal reaches. The
revival in pleasure boats on the canals has brought back a lot of life to the
area.

BARNOLDSWICK

THE LOCKS c1955 / B589007

Grindleton is a classic case of village development: here ancient roads cross, and ribbon building took place along those roads. Many of the old houses were weaver's cottages, built in a time when hand-loom weaving was the major industry in the area. The road from Sawley to Waddington crossed the back road from Clitheroe to Slaidburn here, so the cloth produced from local wool could be taken to the markets and fairs on packhorses. We are looking up from the bottom of the village. 'H Smalley, Grocer & General Dealer, licensed to sell tobacco and cigars', says the sign on the left.

GRINDLETON
THE VILLAGE 1921 / 71175

The post office is on the left with its sign outside. At the time of this photograph, the population of the village had almost halved: local cottage industries had declined, and the arrival of the new mills in the larger towns meant that people flocked there to live and work.

GRINDLETON

THE VILLAGE AND THE POST OFFICE 1921 / 71173

CHATBURN

THE VILLAGE 1921 / 71178

Here we see motorists in the village—they are probably touring the area. The 'burn' part of the name comes from the stream which runs through the village. The 'chat' part is either an Old English personal name 'Ceatta', or the word 'ceat', which means 'piece of wet ground'. In our view we are looking towards the bridge over the burn. The Brown Cow public house is on the right. The village is 400ft above sea level.

CHATBURN

THE VILLAGE 1921 / 71177

We are at the top of the street seen in photograph no 71178. The Black Bull, where the people are standing, was built in 1855; it was a Blackburn Brewery Company pub, and so was The Brown Cow. Can you see the two motor bikes and sidecars in our photograph? These were very popular in the inter-war years with young people, for they were a cheap form of transport. The one nearest the camera seems to have the lady driving and the gentleman in the sidecar.

West Bradford gets its name from being west of the broad, shallow ford of the River Ribble. Again, we see a large painted board; this one proclaims that James Leeming was proprietor of the Three Millstones Inn on the right of our photograph. Eaves Hall, next to the village, is now a country club for the Civil Service Motoring Association. The cottages on the left were a Mission Room before the church of St Catherine was built in 1898.

WEST BRADFORD

THE VILLAGE 1921 / 71150

In this picture we can see the small stream that runs down from Waddington Fell and the Moorcock Inn as it runs right through the centre of the village to join the Ribble. It was at Waddington Old Hall that Henry VI took refuge after leaving Bolton-by-Bowland, and it was here that he was betrayed and captured in nearby Clitheroe Wood. The church of St Helen, with its 15th-century tower, can be seen on the skyline. It was largely rebuilt, but very much in keeping with the original style, in 1901. Many of the Parker family from nearby Browsholme Hall are buried here in the church, and they have their own chapel and pews.

WADDINGTON

THE VILLAGE 1899 / 42914

The apron, or uniform, on the lady in our photograph reminds us that these almshouses were also referred to as Waddington Hospital. The child on the donkey next to her could have been recuperating. In 1706 Robert Parker paid for the building of these almshouses to accommodate twenty-nine widows and spinsters of the parish. They were moved to this site around the village green just over a century later.

WADDINGTON

THE ALMSHOUSES 1899 / 42916

The village of Waddington has won the 'Best Kept Village in Lancashire' title on many occasions. When Queen Elizabeth II came to the throne in 1953, the village erected a Coronation Bridge and laid out Coronation Gardens, which we can see here. The name Waddington means 'the settlement of Wada' (a Saxon chief). Waddow Hall stands close to the village.

WADDINGTON

CORONATION BRIDGE c1960 / W523007

CLITHEROE
BRUNGERLEY BRIDGE 1894 / 34346

Castle Street is Clitheroe's main shopping street. In this photograph the shops look quite busy. Tuesday and Saturday are market days, and the town is packed with villagers coming in from miles around. We can see how the castle dominates the scene, even though only its keep is still standing. The Starkie Arms Hotel is on the far right. Notice the stage-coach arch next to the bay windows.

The Castle Town of Clitheroe

'A township, parochial chapelry, market town, corporate and parliamentary borough', was how Clitheroe was described in 1840. The Honour of Clitheroe, held in medieval times by the de Lacy family, comprised the parishes of Blackburn, Chipping, Ribchester, Bury, Rochdale and the Forest of Bowland; its 28,800 acres were all controlled and run from the Castle. The Charter of Incorporation for Clitheroe was granted in 1147, making it the second oldest town in Lancashire. When there was a major overhaul of the council system in 1974, Clitheroe was the natural headquarters for the newly-formed Ribble Valley Authority.

CLITHEROE

CASTLE STREET 1921 / 71133

We are looking down from the keep of Clitheroe Castle to the town below. Castle Street is in the foreground; it changes to Church Street at the Library (the triangular building with the clock), which was built in 1905. Church Street leads to the large parish church of St Mary Magdalene; its 15th-century tower is topped by a twisted spire, which was added in 1846. The Swan & Royal Hotel stands out on the right of the street, one of the many eating and drinking places on Castle Street.

CLITHEROE

THE VIEW FROM THE CASTLE 1921 / 71129

CLITHEROE

CASTLE STREET 1921 / 71130

We are outside The Swan & Royal. The hotel was originally called The Swan, and was visited by the travel writer John Byng, who in 1792 reported that his bedroom door was broken and that everyone could see him in bed. Apart from the castle, this is the highest part of Clitheroe, 300ft above sea level. It is here that the morris and folk dancing takes place at the Clitheroe Folk Festival.

CLITHEROE

MARKET PLACE 1921 / 71131

Our photographer is standing in Church Street. The early markets were held in this area of the town. The White Lion Hotel on the right is still there today, and so is W D Cunliffe the grocers and bakers. Three doors down on the right, with a horse-drawn vegetable cart in front, is the Victoria Hotel, on the corner of King Street.

The inner keep is on the right, with holes knocked into its 9ft-thick walls. The smallest Norman keep in England, it last saw action at the end of the Civil War, when Colonel Assheton's forces barricaded themselves in the castle. The buildings on the left date from around 1725, when the Crown owned the castle. It has been the property of the Duke of Albermarle, the Duke of Buccleuch and Lord Montagu of Beaulieu. In 1919, amid the pain and sadness after the First World War, the people of Clitheroe raised £15,000 to buy the Castle and its grounds, and a Garden of Remembrance was laid out.

CLITHEROE
THE CASTLE 1927 / 80535

We are looking north towards Kemple End. The sizeable railway sidings that we can see here denote how important Clitheroe was as a distribution centre for this part of the Ribble Valley. After the sheep market on Monday and livestock markets on Tuesday and Friday, animals were transported all over Lancashire. The origin of the name Clitheroe is surrounded by doubt and mystery. The 'oe' at the end comes from the Old English 'hoh', meaning a hill or promontory. The 'Clith' part could come from OE 'clyde', stones or rocky.

CLITHEROE

FROM THE CASTLE 1927 / 80530

Worston once stood astride the main A59 road, but now it is happy to be a quiet backwater in the shadow of Pendle. This sleepy scene is typical of the lovely villages in the area.

Around the Hill named Pendle

Though parts of Pendle Hill reach over 1,900ft, it never quite makes it to 2,000 feet—the height when a hill becomes a mountain. Because of the famous Pendle witch trials in 1612, the hill has gained a reputation for sorcery and evil deeds. Those who know the area treat these superstitious tales with a pinch of salt, but they do not deny that the quick changes in weather, which bring down the clouds over the hill, certainly add to the brooding mystery of Pendle Hill. The beauty of the place inspired George Fox, the founder of the Quaker movement, when he was here in the mid-15th century, and many poets have written about this lovely area.

WORSTON

THE VILLAGE 1921 / 71160

45

Children pose near the small bridge over Downham Beck, a brook which runs through the heart of the village. Downham is another example of a village which was tightly controlled by the lords of the manor, who refused to let industry into the village. St Leonard's Church, which we can see on the left in the background, has been rebuilt twice. Parts of it date from the 1400s, and the three bells are said to have come from the Abbey after it was pulled down.

DOWNHAM

THE VILLAGE 1894 / 34357

The name Downham means 'dwelling by the hill'—the hill is obviously Pendle, which can be seen in the background. This photograph is unfortunate in that it makes the village look a little ramshackle, but in fact it was rather smart. The Asshetons looked after their village. Almost all the villagers had jobs on the estate. The Roman road from Ribchester to Ikley passes through Downham Park at the end of the village. The grave of Roman soldiers killed in a skirmish with the Brigantes is said to be marked with a large stone to the left of the gates to the Hall.

DOWNHAM
THE VILLAGE 1895 / 35716

DOWNHAM

THE POST OFFICE AND THE OLD STOCKS 1921 / 71190

*Here we see the Post Office complete with children and a horse and trap out-
side. On the right an old sycamore tree shades what is left of the village
stocks. The film 'Whistle Down The Wind' with Hayley Mills was filmed
in and around Downham village.*

This posed picture shows the lower part of the village. The 15th-century tower of the village church is peeping out on the skyline on the left. The church has some very fierce-looking gargoyles; it is the last resting-place of many of the Assheton family, who have their own chapel and vault there.

DOWNHAM

THE VILLAGE 1921 / 71189

This is the T-junction at the centre of Hurst Green. This stretch of road has a history all of its own. In 1826 J C Macadam laid a new road surface here as a trial. Hundreds of locals came to see it, and 'tarmacadam' became a huge success. This is the Shirburne's village; it was started by the family to house estate workers, and servants from nearby Stonyhurst, whose entrance is on the left. The Eagle & Child Inn reflects a marriage with the Stanley family, and the Shirburne Arms (formerly the Three Fishes) is just out of sight on the right.

HURST GREEN

THE CROSS c1950 / H445011

51

The house, which was at one time the largest building in the north of England, was built by Sir Nicolas Sherburn (Shirburn) around 1690. The estate was left to a cousin (named Weld) who gave it to the Jesuits in 1794. The estate is over 2,000 acres, much of which is farmed. The church of St Peter can be seen to the right of the picture. The college has a library that contains mementoes of many famous people, including Bonnie Prince Charlie and Mary Queen of Scots.

STONYHURST COLLEGE

1899 / 43489

Today, Little Mitton Hall is an hotel. Mitton means 'the village where the streams meet'. The Hodder and the Ribble meet here, and that is what gave the area its name. Great Mitton is on the north bank of the river, and Little, or Lower Mitton on the south bank, with the River Ribble (which we can see here) in between.

LITTLE MITTON

THE HALL 1894 / 34344

The T-junction and church are just ahead. St Mary and All Saints has ancient crosses in the churchyard and a thousand years of history. In the grounds there is a sundial dating from the 1700s. The biggest problem for visitors to Whalley today is finding a space to park. Whalley Abbey and its grounds have passed through many hands since being seized by Henry VIII, but it is now back in the hands of the church. Much of the faric from the demolished abbey found its way into the church, including the misericords.

WHALLEY
ACCRINGTON ROAD 1901 / 47063

Here we have a grand view of the railway arches heading out of Whalley. The railway arrived in the village in 1850, and the 600yd-long viaduct carries the Blackburn to Clitheroe line at a height of 70ft. Whalley is just a village, though a large one; it is always high on the best-kept village awards list, a title which it has won in the past. The last Abbot of Whalley, a Cistercian monk, is thought to be buried in the parish church after being hung for opposing Henry VIII.

WHALLEY

BROAD LANE 1906 / 54210

Whalley means 'the clearing or field by the hill', and we can see how close the hill known as Whalley Nab is. Here in the main street, a policeman stands on traffic duty at the junction with Accrington Road outside the Whalley Arms. The church here was once the mother church for half of Lancashire (47 townships and three large villages). On King Street and the corner of Station Road is an old cricket square, said to be where the first Lancashire versus Yorkshire match was played.

WHALLEY

KING STREET 1921 / 71116

This photograph was taken from Wesley Street. It was only a mile away that George Fox, the Quaker, stood on the 'nick' of Pendle in 1652 and declared himself moved to start a religious order, the Society of Friends. Sabden is unique in that it was almost an industrial village. It had six mills at one time, and yet it sits astride the old pack-horse trails in a green and remote area within Pendle's rim. It will always be connected with Richard Cobden, the reformer, who owned one of the mills here. Sabden was noted for its production of gentlemen's handkerchiefs for a time. The village 'Treacle Mine' was a well, or spring, whose water was used to 'treat all' complaints.

SABDEN

THE WESLEYAN CHURCH AND WESLEY STREET c1960 / S691011

PENDLETON

THE VILLAGE 1921 / 71164

Pendleton nestles right in the shadow of Pendle Hill: in fact, the name means 'the houses on Pendle'. Owned for centuries by the Aspinall family, Pendleton was an old village when the Domesday Book was compiled. With its stream running down the middle of the village, Pendleton presents an idyllic picture.

The houses here are built of local stone. The stream meanders through the
centre of the village, and local children play pooh sticks and just watch the
stream. The fortunes of the village have fluctated with time, and week-enders
and in-comers now make up a large part of the old village. The village was
once nicknamed 'the goose village', because it was said that geese from
Pendleton tasted better than any others in Lancashire.

PENDLETON

THE VILLAGE 1921 / 71165

The church is dedicated to St Wilfrid, the Archbishop of York in the 660s. Wilfrid is a northern dedication, and usually denotes an ancient church. Ribchester was once a Roman fort (Bremetennacum), and it was situated by an important ford of the River Ribble. In front of the church is the graveyard; here it is not looking at its best, and very uneven. The fact that the churchyard is circular suggests that it follows the line of some earlier Roman structure. Nearby is Ribchester Museum, which is devoted to the Romans who lived here more than 1,500 years ago.

RIBCHESTER

THE CHURCH 1894 / 34325

The oldest building in Colne is the church. St Bartholomew's dates from the 1200s, and much of the 62ft tower is original. The church has stocks and a charnel house in the graveyard. The name Colne means 'roaring river'.

Colne Water
and the
River Calder

We move to the third of our three rivers, and go high into the hills to find Colne Water. The area used to be known as Marsden. Great Marsden covers what is now called Colne, and Little Marsden was known as Nelson down to Reedley. Walverton Water ran between the two Marsdens. The district was entirely dependent on agriculture two hundred years ago; it slowly turned to the wool industry, then to cotton, and now it has a mixture of light and heavy industry and engineering. Coal mining was once a prosperous industry here.

COLNE

THE CHURCH c1955 / C600020

63

The story of how the town got its name is an unusual one. When the railway arrived, a station was built here at Marsden. There was another Marsden just a few miles up the line in Yorkshire, so a railway official gave the station the name of the inn that was next to the station. This inn was called The Lord Nelson, after the famous admiral. The station's name was was shortened to Nelson to make the sign smaller, and the whole area has been known as Nelson ever since.

NELSON

MANCHESTER ROAD c1955 / N146011

The Borough Hotel is on the right of our photograph;
this was a Dutton House. Woolworth's is a little further
up the street. The Corporation once operated a light
railway to Barrowford and Colne from here.

NELSON

On the right is the United Free Methodist Church, which opened in 1869, and facing it on the left is Burnley Town Hall. The Town Hall was built in 1888; it was completed in the October of that year to a design by Holton & Fox of Dewsbury, at a cost of £50,000. It is built of Yorkshire stone in a classical Renaissance style.

Burnley

Burnley means 'the place by the river Brun'; the town snuggles in a valley between the rivers Calder and Brun. As with so many other towns in the area, it was the Leeds and Liverpool canal which brought about the growth of Burnley, and there is a large piece of that canal history alive and well at the Weaver's Triangle on the Burnley Wharf, Manchester Road. There were once 200 mills and industrial chimneys pouring smoke into the air of Burnley. There were also once over 80 coal mines in the area, but all have now gone; the last one, Hapton Valley, closed in 1982.

BURNLEY

MANCHESTER ROAD 1895 / 35789

*The Institute was opened in 1855 by Colonel Charles Townley; it was a
haven for apprentices taking on night-school to further their careers, and for
youngsters wanting to better themselves. It is still there today as an Arts
Centre and the Tourist Information Centre. Burnley Town Hall peeps out
from behind the Institute. It became the New Empress Night Club in 1963,
and after that a Bingo Hall. Queen Elizabeth II came and re-opened the
restored, re-designed Mechanics Institute on 12 November 1987.*

BURNLEY

THE MECHANICS' INSTITUTE 1895 / 35787

Duke Bar is on the outskirts of Burnley. The Duke of York public house can be seen in the centre of our picture. Burnley was one of the few towns where steam trams were employed after the horse buses and before the electric trams that the corporation introduced in the early 1900s. Note the wonderfully-lettered sign for the Duke Bar Bottle Stores on the left of the picture, which promotes 'Grimshaw's Lancastrian Ales & Stout'. The railway arrived in Burnley from Accrington in September 1848, and six months later the line went on to Colne. The railway had a large impact on the town, especially as there was so much coal mining in the area.

BURNLEY

DUKE BAR 1906 / 54183

Scott Park was opened on 18 August 1895; it was named after
Alderman Scott, who had died in 1891 leaving £10,000 in his
will to open a public park. In this photograph it looks rather new and
un-developed, as indeed it was at this time. Some said that Burnley
did not need parks, as the Pennines of South Lancashire are only ten
minutes away, and some lovely countryside surrounds the town.

BURNLEY
SCOTT PARK 1896 / 37408

The castellated entrance to Townley Hall, on the A671 Todmorden Road at Burnley Wood, was photographed when it was still a private estate. The Townley family owned the hall for over 500 years; it was given to the people of Burnley by the last occupant, Lady O'Hagan, the widow of Lord O'Hagan, former Lord Chancellor of Ireland. Born Alice Mary Townley, she was tireless in her work for the people of Burnley, especially the less fortunate. In March 1902 she sold the hall and its 62 acres to Burnley for the very low price of £17,500, and paid for the art gallery it housed.

BURNLEY

TOWNLEY PARK GATE 1895 / 35800

BURNLEY

TOWNLEY HALL 1906 / 54201

Townley Hall was first opened to the people of Burnley on 20 May 1903. Some parts of the south-east wing go back to the 14th century, and the clock over the entrance has been marking the passing of time for about 350 years. Richard Townley re-built the central great hall in 1725. The diamonds in the Hall's crown are the chapel and its carved altar piece in a room built entirely of oak.

Blackburn Road is at the very heart of the town. The first building on the right is the Market Hall, and next to that, in the centre of our photograph, is the Town Hall.

Around Accrington

The name Accrington means 'community where the acorns grow'. Acorns were the main source of food for pigs in Norman England, and pigs were an important source of food for many Lancashire villages. The name was written as 'Akarington' in 1194 and 'Acrinton' in 1277. The town grew up on the edge of the Rossendale Forrest. In 1801, Accrington was just a growing village with a population of under 3,000. Before the start of the Great War in 1914, it was an industrial town of over 45,000 people. In 1974, the Municipal Borough of Hyndburn was formed by amalgamating Accrington with five other towns.

ACCRINGTON

BLACKBURN ROAD 1897 / 40116

Here we see a close-up view of the Market Hall with its imposing front and large statues mounted over the entrance. There was a corn market in Accrington as far back as the 16th century. This Market Hall was opened on 23 October 1868 by Samuel Dugdale, Chairman of the local Board of Health. It contained 80 permanent stalls and shops, plus 23 lock-ups in the basement, served by lifts, for the use of the stall-holders. Market days were Tuesday, Friday and Saturday. Early closing day was Wednesday.

ACCRINGTON

MARKET HALL 1897 / 40117

This photograph was taken from outside the Market Hall looking down Blackburn Road towards its junction with Abbey Street. Boots & David Lewis had led the way by being cash-only shops; by 1899, the trend of negotiating over a reduction in the marked price had almost died out. Here we see a Cash Clothing shop on the left, with its 'ready money bargains' piled high in the windows. 'Drink Altham's 2/4d Tea', proclaims the banner further down the street.

ACCRINGTON

BLACKBURN ROAD 1899 / 43496

The need for Cottage Hospitals was great a century ago, but with the advent of more advanced equipment and specialised nursing, these cottage hospitals, like the isolation hospitals, closed down. Accrington Victoria Hospital took the place of this building, and later a lot of the services were moved to Burnley General Hospital.

ACCRINGTON

THE COTTAGE HOSPITAL 1899 / 43505

The railway line to Huncoat and Burnley crosses the road here. There was at one time another line down to Rawtenstall, joining what is now the East Lancashire Preserved Railway. As well as having three railway lines, the town also had three turnpike roads. They were the Whalley to Manchester Road (1790), now Abbey Street; the Blackburn Road (1826-7); and the road to Burnley (1838).

ACCRINGTON

BLACKBURN ROAD c1915 / A19004

It is interesting to compare this photograph with picture no 40116 on pages 74 to 75, which was taken from nearly the same spot, but 50 years earlier. The street is still cobbled, but the tram lines have gone. Our 'Cash Clothing' shop is now just an ordinary shop (next to the Savoy Cafe on the right). It looks like a good solid Silver Cross pram parked outside the tobacconist's on the left of our photograph.

ACCRINGTON
BLACKBURN ROAD c1955 / A19013

Stanhill is a small community on one of the B-roads between Oswaldtwistle and Blackburn. It was in this building in 1764 that James Hargreaves lived when he invented the Spinning Jenny. Because of his new invention and the new mechanisation it brought about, many people were forced out of their rural homes to work in the factories, and he was forced out of this house and the area. Apart from the ice cream sign and the newspaper advertising board ('Hollywood stars revolt'), the scene could have been anything up to 50 years earlier. There are a lot of these small villages in this hilly agricultural area.

STANHILL
THE POST OFFICE c1955 / s814003

STANHILL

STANHILL ROAD c1955 / s814004

This photograph shows how near the hills and open countryside are to the towns around here. Oswaldtwistle Moor, to the south of the town, is a lovely unspoilt area of outstanding beauty. 'The 'twist', or meeting of rivers, where Oswald lives' is how the town gets its name.

Great Harwood lies to the north of Accrington, and commands a lovely part of the Hyndburn Valley. Dominating the east on a hill next to Great Harwood is the Roman Catholic Church of St Hubert, an unusual dedication. It is a large church, and though not as ancient as its neighbour St Bartholomew's, it has some very fine stained glass windows.

GREAT HARWOOD

THE ROMAN CATHOLIC CHURCH

1898 / 40143

Here we have a busy and bustling view of Northgate. The Market Hall and its tower are on the right of our picture, and the square, solid Town Hall is at the side of it. The Market House, as it was called, opened on 28 January 1848. It opened every day except Sunday, and was famous for stalls selling black puddings and sarsparilla. Unfortunately, the old Market House and Clock Tower were cleared away in the 1960s when the new Market Hall opened.

Blackburn and Darwen

Blackburn means 'on the black stream'. The town guards the entrances to the river valleys we have been looking at in earlier pages - the Ribble, the Hyndeburn and the Hodder - and was the starting point for journeys into these areas and over to Yorkshire. For over a century, Blackburn was known as 'the biggest weaving town in the world'; it boasted over 80,000 looms in 130 mills. It was the arrival of the Leeds/Liverpool canal in 1810 that turned a hand-loom cottage industry into the giant of the Industrial Revolution. Coal was mined in Darwen, and there was an alum mine at Pleasington.

BLACKBURN

THE MARKET AND TOWN HALL
1894 / 34307

When this photograph was taken, Blackburn had two markets, the indoor
market and an open air one, held every Wednesday and Saturday. This
photograph shows the open market in New Market Street. Here we see the
Market Hall (or House) from the rear, and the back of the Town Hall; its
20ft-high wall guards a courtyard. It was the Market Square that hosted
the Blackburn Fair, which was held by Charter every Easter Monday, and
then on 11 and 12 May, and also the Winter Fair every 17 October.

BLACKBURN

THE MARKET 1894 / 34306

Blackburn possessed six parks, but Corporation Park was the one laid out on clear Victorian lines. Sixty acres were transformed with terraced walks, as we see here. A magnificent palm house, lake and conservatory were also part of this lovely park. Over 60,000 people turned up to see it opened on 23 October 1857. The making of the park provided work for many of the unemployed cotton workers. Notice that every single person in our photograph, from the youngest to the oldest, is wearing a hat. Top hats, boaters, bowlers, billy cocks and bonnets—they are all here.

BLACKBURN

CORPORATION PARK 1895 / 35729

The shops behind the big lamp in the centre of the road are interesting. Next to the draper's shop on the left is Walmsley's Stationers and Bookshop. The large window proudly proclaims that they have a Bible and Prayer Book Department. The horse-drawn tram heads off towards the Town Hall. The Sudell family can be traced back to the reign of Edward VI. They owned land in Blackburn and out at Oozebooth. The family built a large town house on King Street. They also built a large warehouse, and Sudell Court and Sudell's Yard appeared round it. Henry Sudell, the last of the family to live in Blackburn, enclosed Woodfold Park, and built the Hall there.

BLACKBURN
SUDELL CROSS 1895 / 35726

Here we see the grand facade of the Blackburn Exchange & Reading Room, which opened in April 1865. It was known later as the Cotton Exchange. The building, at least the front, is still there today, and is a cinema. Blackburn had had three local newspapers by the time the Reading Room opened. The 'Blackburn Mail' started in 1793; the 'Blackburn Alfred' newspaper was first published in 1832; and the 'Blackburn Times' was first issued on 2 June 1855.

BLACKBURN

THE EXCHANGE 1899 / 43478

BLACKBURN

SALFORD BRIDGE 1899 / 43476

This is where the old pack horse trail to Accrington and the east crossed the
River Blakewater in a shallow ford. By the time our photograph was taken, the
river was covered over for over 1,000ft, and Salford Bridge was technically
420ft-wide. We can see the Bay Horse Hotel on the right, with the Royal
Commercial Hotel behind it.

Here we see the entrance lodge to Corporation Park. No expense was spared in the making of the park and its lodge. The Borough coat of arms and its motto, 'Arte et Labore', is cut into the stone, along with the name of the park over the entrance arch. In the 1950s over 35% of jobs in Blackburn were in engineering, 20% in textiles, and the rest in paper, beer and plastics.

BLACKBURN

CORPORATION PARK 1923 / 74052

Blackburn's Public Hall opened in 1923. The
Sessions House is just beyond it on the right.
Now called King George's Hall, it is still one
of the centres of entertainment in Blackburn.

BLACKBURN

THE PUBLIC HALL AND THE SESSIONS HOUSE 1923 / 74070

Here we see an almost deserted Queen's Park, with just one customer for a rowing boat on the park's lake. The park opened on 20 June 1887 in Queen Victoria's Jubilee year.

BLACKBURN

QUEEN'S PARK LAKE 1923 / 74051

The foundation stone for the Towen Hall was laid on 29 October 1852 by Joseph Fielden, and it was opened on 30 October 1856. The total cost was £29,428 16s 3d. The clock tower and the Market Hall are still present in our photograph, but they were not to last for long. Blackburn became a County Borough in 1888. On 5 November 1925 the Blackburn Church Diocese was founded, and the parish church became a Cathedral.

BLACKBURN

THE TOWN HALL c1955 / B111003

This photograph captures the great changes that were going on in Blackburn during the post-war period. Blackburn had started to expand with the canal age. Then, in 1797, its first turnpike opened, connecting it with Bolton. In 1770 there were 5,000 people living in the town, and by 1811 there were 15,083, three times that number; by 1835 the population had doubled again. The railway to Preston opened in 1846, but the station we see here did not open until 12 September 1886.

BLACKBURN

THE BOULEVARD c1955 / B111034

An ornate 19th-century fountain graces the park. This is one of three parks in Darwen, all very different. Sunnyhurst Wood is a Nature Reserve; Sunnyhurst Brook runs through it to join the River Darwen that gave the town its name. Bold Venture Park is a disused quarry, with a lake and a picturesque waterfall. Whitehall Park has always been noted for its floral displays, and the rhododendrons make a great show in the late Spring.

DARWEN

WHITEHALL PARK 1895 / 35738

This view from the top of Whitehall Park looks over the flower beds to Darwen beyond. We can make out quite a few of the mill chimneys, but not the most famous of them all, the square 300ft India Mill chimney. Built of local brick with wide stone viewing balconies, it is modelled on the bell-tower of St Marks Square in Venice, and it took fourteen years to build. The River Darwen (a Celtic name) is only 15 miles long before it joins the Ribble near Preston.

DARWEN

WHITEHALL PARK 1896 / 35735

The Circus, in the town centre, is where five roads meet. It has the usual mixture of banks and public houses on its corners. A National Savings Centre is tucked away on the left of our picture, and the Millstone Hotel is at the far side. Note the very primitive Belisha beacon crossings to guide pedestrians across the large open area.

DARWEN

THE CIRCUS c1955 / D8010

The Town Hall and the Market Hall are on the right. Known as Over Darwen, this was a quarrying and agricultural area before turning to calico printing, weaving and paper making. On the skyline you can see Darwen Tower. Built in honour of the Diamond Jubilee of Queen Victoria in 1897, the 85ft tower is 1,300ft above sea level. There is a viewing platform at the top which gives magnificent views over the moors around.

DARWEN
THE MARKET HALL c1955 / D8012

Turton Tower lies four miles south of Darwen, and four miles north-east of Bolton. The villages of Turton and Turton Bottoms are next to the Tower. Turton Tower is basically two buildings, a pele tower dating from the 1100s, modernised around 1450, and a farm house or family hall, added in the late 14th century. In 1930 the hall was sold to the local authorities, and Turton Tower is now open to the public; it is well worth a visit.

TURTON TOWER

1897 / 40106

Before 1892, all ships delivering to Preston would use the riverside for loading and unloading. The year 1892 saw the opening of the Albert Edward Dock Basin: here we see that dock just a year later. Its success can be measured by the large number of ships tied up there. Note how rural the area behind the quay looks—today, it is a shopping complex with fast food outlets.

Proud Preston

Preston (which means 'the priest's town') stands on the River Ribble. It is famous for its Guilds, and the Preston Guild Celebrations are held every twenty years. The town is just fifteen miles from open sea, near enough to have docks; Preston has been used as a port since 1360. While Preston does not mark the end of the Ribble, it marks the end of our journey: we have followed the river down from the Pennines, and have seen it pick up all those other rivers on the way - the Calder, the Hodder, the Douglas and many more smaller rivulets that pour into the Ribble. By the time the Ribble reaches Preston it is a deep, mighty river, well able to sustain sea-going vessels.

PRESTON

THE DOCKS 1893 / 33097

In 1792, a company was formed by Lancaster merchants to build a canal; they saw it as a way of getting cheap coal from Wigan and transporting other goods out into towns in the heart of Lancashire. Unfortunately, the company ran out of money, the aqueduct over the River Ribble was put on hold, and a cheaper alternative, a tramway between the north and south sections, was built. Here we see the tram bridge, which was built in 1803. Trams had ceased running over this bridge in 1879.

PRESTON

OLD TRAM BRIDGE OVER THE RIVER RIBBLE 1893 / 33100

The hotel was built by the London and North Western Railway Company for travellers from London to Scotland. At that time, around 1860, it was considered bad for your health to attempt the whole journey without an overnight stop half-way, which happened to be at Preston. The Park Hotel cost £46,000 to build; it was designed by Mr A Mitchell.

PRESTON

AVENHAM PARK AND THE PARK HOTEL 1893 / 33094

This bridge is a railway bridge, and is now part of the west coast main line. Another railway bridge (to Blackburn) can be seen in the distance. Preston was the centre of a wheel of railway transport: spokes went off to Blackpool, Lancaster, Blackburn, Manchester, London, Liverpool and Southport. As we can see, the river was used for pleasure. Boats could be hired from the Pleasure Boat Inn, which is on the left.

PRESTON

THE BRIDGE OVER THE RIBBLE 1903 / 50077

The building on the left of our photograph was not just the
Art Gallery, but also the Harris Public Library and Museum;
it was opened in 1893 as a library, but was not in full use
until 1896. The Town Hall, designed by Sir Gilbert Scott,
was started in 1862. It burnt down in 1947, and after much
debate, the ruins were cleared away in the early 1960s.

PRESTON

THE TOWN HALL, ART GALLERY AND LIBRARY 1903 / 50084

The tower with its clock belongs to the Preston Baptist Church; the Town Hall spire can be seen further up Fishergate. There is an interesting diversity of shops, from a plumber's to the Cocoa Rooms - this has always been Preston's main shopping street.

PRESTON

FISHERGATE 1903 / 50065

III

The home of the de Hoghton family, the house (which is still there today) was mainly built in the reign of Elizabeth I. In the early 14th century, Sir Richard Hoghton and his wife, Sybilla de Lea, presided over an estate which was was already over 40,000 acres. The Tower will always be associated with the visit of James I when he dubbed a simple loin of beef 'Sir Loin'. Thomas Hoghton built most of what we see here in 1565. The house was never fortified, so it escaped destruction by Cromwell. Today it is open to the public.

HOGHTON

HOGHTON TOWER 1895 / 35719

At this time, local industry was closing down; Bacup, which was off the beaten track, was looking for residents to commute to work in Burnley, Manchester or other towns. The town stands on the young River Irwell, in the Rossendale Valley—the name Bacup means 'in the valley by the bridge'. Bacup is the home of the famous Britannia Coconut Dancers. The whole area was also famous for the manufacture of slippers.

BACUP

ST JAMES STREET 1961 / B588050

Chorley, Heading South

This is Chorley's main street, the A6, Lancashire's main north to south road; it used to get very busy in the summer. Our photograph was taken before the M6 or the Chorley by-pass opened—Chorley was troubled by heavy traffic for many years. Bleasdale's furniture shop and Yates's Wine Lodge are on the left, and Mangnells and E R Booth are on the right.

CHORLEY

MARKET STREET c1965 / C537055

CHORLEY

CHAPEL STREET c1965 / C537018

This photograph was taken further up the street from no C537055. The shops on the left bring back many memories, and F W Woolworth is there as well. Chorley Town Hall, with its clock and spire, show up (right) at the north end of the street. Chorley gets its name from the smallish but charming River Chor, which runs north of the market town.

CHORLEY

MARKET STREET c1960 / C537016

The hall, parts of which date from 1550, has been re-built and added to over the years. It was only two stories high when it was first built—the long gallery and the balustraded top were added in 1685. The Hall belonged to the Charnock, the Brooke and the Parker families before Reginald Tatton gave it to the town as part of a memorial to the local men who gave their lives in the First World War. It was formally handed over in February 1922, and it opened as a museum on 31 May 1924.

CHORLEY

ASTLEY HALL c1960 / c537037

Chorley's oldest building is the parish church of St Lawrence, which was built in the 14th century. The centre aisle is the original church; the two side aisles were added in c1860.

CHORLEY

THE PARISH CHURCH c1965 / C537057

ADLINGTON

MARKET STREET c1960 / A338008

A bread delivery van and some local traffic make Adlington look busy. The name of the village comes from an Old English personal name, Aethel, meaning 'a noble friend'.

INDEX

PLEASE HELP US BRING FRITH'S PHOTOGRAPHS TO LIFE

Our authors do their best to recount the history of the places they write about. They give insights into how particular towns and villages developed, they describe the architecture of streets and buildings, and they discuss the lives of famous people who lived there. But however knowledgeable our authors are, the story they tell is necessarily incomplete.

Frith's photographs are so much more than plain historical documents. They are living proofs of the flow of human life down the generations. They show real people at real moments in history; and each of those people is the son or daughter of someone, the brother or sister, aunt or uncle, grandfather or grandmother of someone else. All of them lived, worked and played in the streets depicted in Frith's photographs.

We would be grateful if you would tell us about the many places shown in our photographs—the streets with their buildings, shops, businesses and industries. Describe your own memories of life in those streets: what it was like growing up there, who ran the local shop and what shopping was like years ago; if your workplace is shown tell us about your working day and what the building is used for now. With your help more and more Frith photographs can be brought to life, and vital memories preserved for posterity.

We will gradually add your comments and stories to the archive for the benefit of historians of the future. Wherever possible, we will try to include some of your comments in future editions of our books. Moreover, if you spot errors in dates, titles or other facts, please let us know, because our archive records are not always completely accurate—they rely on 150 years of human endeavour and hand-compiled records.

So please write, fax or email us with your stories and memories. Thank you!

CHOOSE ANY PHOTOGRAPH FROM THIS BOOK

for your FREE Mounted Print. Order further prints at half price

Fill in and cut out the voucher on the next page and return it with your remittance for £2.50 for postage, packing and handling to UK addresses (US $5.00 for USA and Canada). For all other overseas addresses include £5.00 post and handling.
Choose any photograph included in this book. Make sure you quote its unique reference number eg. 42365 (it is mentioned after the photograph date. 1890 / 42365). Your SEPIA print will be approx 12" x 8" and mounted in a cream mount with a burgundy rule line (overall size 14" x 11").

Mounted Print
Overall size 14 x 11 inches

Order additional Mounted Prints at HALF PRICE - If you would like to order more Frith prints from this book, possibly as gifts for friends and family, you can buy them at half price (with no extra postage and handling costs) - only £7.49 each (UK orders), US $14.99 each (USA and Canada).

---

* IMPORTANT!

These special prices are only available if you order at the same time as you order your free mounted print. You must use the ORIGINAL VOUCHER on the facing page (no copies permitted). We can only despatch to one address.

Have your Mounted Prints framed (UK orders only) - For an extra £14.95 per print you can have your mounted print(s) framed in an elegant polished wood and gilt moulding, overall size 16" x 13" (no additional postage).

FRITH PRODUCTS AND SERVICES

All Frith photographs are available for you to buy as framed or mounted prints. From time to time, other illustrated items such as Address Books, Calendars, Table Mats are also available. Already, almost 50,000 Frith archive photographs can be viewed and purchased on the internet through the Frith website.

For more detailed information on Frith companies and products, visit

www.francisfrith.co.uk

For further information, trade, or author enquiries, contact:

The Francis Frith Collection, Frith's Barn, Teffont, Salisbury SP3 5QP
Tel: +44 (0) 1722 716 376 Fax: +44 (0) 1722 716 881 Email: sales@francisfrith.co.uk